FOR YOUR HOME

FAMILY ROOMS

FOR YOUR HOME

FAMILY ROOMS

CANDACE ORD MANROE

Little, Brown and Company
Boston   New York   Toronto   London

DEDICATION

FOR MEAGAN AND DREW

First Edition

ISBN 0-316-65210-5

Library of Congress Catalogue Card Number 93-81323

A FRIEDMAN GROUP BOOK

10 9 8 7 6 5 4 3 2 1

Published simultaneously in Canada by Little, Brown & Company (Canada) Limited

FOR YOUR HOME: FAMILY ROOMS
was prepared and produced by
Michael Friedman Publishing Group, Inc.
15 West 26th Street
New York, New York 10010

Editor: Sharyn Rosart
Art Director: Jeff Batzli
Designers: Patrick McCarthy and Lynne Yeamans
Photography Editor: Jennifer Crowe McMichael

Color separations by Fine Arts Repro House Co., Ltd.
Printed and bound in China by Leefung-Asco Printers Ltd.

TABLE OF CONTENTS

INTRODUCTION

By virtue of its name, the family room is a life-style indicator. Unlike the bedroom, bathroom, kitchen, or living room, the family room points not so much to a specific, task-oriented function as to an informal, comfortable approach to living in the home that centers around family togetherness. The particular activities pursued in the family room are of less importance than the deeper value statement the room suggests: the importance of gathering, for whatever purpose, in a space designated specifically for those individuals who share the community life defined as a family.

Today, with "family values" having become a buzzword in our culture, the emphasis on home and family has never been stronger. The notion of "cocooning"—nestling into the safety and sanctuary of the home as the preferred place for spending leisure time, as opposed to seeking entertainment and diversion outside the home—emerged in the late 1980s. The momentum continues to grow, as the popularity of home entertaining and the booming home video business illustrate. Not since the 1950s have family rooms been of greater importance in planning and designing the home than they are today.

Not only does the family room in general serve as a life-style barometer for the 1990s; in its specific forms and variations, it reflects the development of other cultural phenomena in our society. This is especially true of home electronics, whose breakneck pace of technological development has left its indelible mark on the family room. To keep up, the family room must adapt and change its own form.

The family room of the 1950s had that epoch's marvel, the television, as its focal point. If the TV wasn't encased in its own cabinet as a freestanding piece of furniture, it usually rested on a TV stand or table. Of secondary importance was the hi-fi, which also was self-contained as a console model. In contrast, the family room of the 1990s is likely to have an entire home media center or even home theater as its entertainment source, with components replacing casegoods and with state-of-the-art audio

Left: PRECONCEIVED NOTIONS OF THE TRADITIONAL DEN UNDERGO RADICAL RETHINKING IN THIS SPACE: ITS FIREPLACE AND LOCATION IN THE BACK OF THE HOME MAKE THIS ROOM A DEN BY DEFINITION, BUT EASY STEREOTYPING OF THE SPACE STOPS HERE. THE CLEAN, CONTEMPORARY ROOM IS THE ANTITHESIS OF THE WOODY, RUGGED PROTOTYPE DEN. FROM THE GEOMETRIC, SCULPTED DOORWAY TO THE BLACK-TILED CEILING, THIS DEN IS A DRAMATIC EXPRESSION OF ITS OWNERS' SOPHISTICATED, CONTEMPORARY SENSIBILITIES.

equipment, storage capacity for videos, CDs, and tapes, and perhaps even a movie screen for TV and video viewing, as well as a home computer.

Obviously, these changes over four decades have necessitated some revision in how the family room is designed. The '50s family room was fine for a console TV and hi-fi; it may not accommodate the accoutrements of a fully-equipped 1990s home entertainment system, which typically requires an entire wall of cabinet or shelf space. As much as any area of the home, the family room is a case of form following function.

The family room is an invention that originated in the post–World War II boom era. It was prefigured in Victorian times, when homes were commonly designed with double parlors—one for receiving guests and another for the privacy of the family. For large occasions, the two parlors could be opened up. But even in the family parlor, an abiding formality reigned, both in the architecture and the furnishings, as well as in the location of the room toward the front of the dwelling.

After World War I, families began to move to the suburbs, and the houses they built changed, becoming less formal. By World War II, this trend had become a way of life, with affordable housing transforming suburbia into the mecca of family life. The new suburban homes reflected a significantly less formal life-style characterized by backyard barbecues and neighborhood progressive suppers, in which casseroles replaced the more elegant, multi-course dinners of years gone by. This new life-style pivoted on the backyard, leading home owners to create a casual living space just off the back of the house that opened onto the yard. The traditional family room, often called a den, was the result. Not only did the room face the yard, but in another practical consideration, it was also usually adjacent to the kitchen for easy interaction between the two hubs. Another feature typical of this new room was a fireplace, which permitted the family to huddle snugly in the room, watching TV, reading, or simply communing.

In the 1970s, the family room took another turn, in some homes evolving into the "great room." This space's prototype dates back even before the Victorian era, to colonial times, when the "keeping room" was the central, most utilized space. This was the original multipurpose room, serving as both kitchen and living room, with the hearth as the focal point for cooking, staying warm, and socializing.

Like the keeping room, the great room usually incorporates a dining table and opens onto the kitchen, with no visual barriers separating the two spaces. Unlike the early

keeping room, which tended to be dark, with only a few small windows (to help keep warmth indoors), the great room often embraces impressive outdoor views through large expanses of glass, thanks to improved insulation and climate-controlled heating and cooling.

Today's family room can take at least four distinct forms, with much overlap and many variations: the traditional den, cozy with its fireplace and back-of-the-house location; the great room, larger and more open than the den, incorporating an eating table and often capturing vistas through large windows or glass doors; the recreation room, which may have traditional play equipment such as dart boards, as well as electronic entertainment, and which is frequently located in the basement; and finally, the home media center, which may be found in any room, even in a spare bedroom, that has been enlisted for this specialized service as a family room.

Whichever form the family room assumes, one theme remains constant: Of all the rooms in the home, the family room is the space that exudes warmth and a beckoning comfort. This is the place where the veil is lifted and the real personalities of the home owners are revealed. It is the room where family members gather to enjoy each other's company and it is notable for its absence of pretense, for its kick-your-shoes-off style. In the anatomy of the home, the family room is the heart.

Above: A COMMONSENSE APPROACH TO DESIGNING THE DEN IS TO GO WITH THE HOME'S PERVADING ARCHITECTURAL STYLE. IN THIS CASE, THE ARCHITECTURE IS REGIONAL, CELEBRATING A SOUTHWESTERN INFLUENCE. THE DEN INCORPORATES THAT STYLE'S CHARACTERISTIC JUXTAPOSITION OF RUGGED BEAMS AND CLEAN, WHITE WALLS; OF DECORATIVE TILES AT THE FIREPLACE AND SPARE ACCESSORIES (SUCH AS THE COW SKULL ABOVE); AND OF COMFORT ARTICULATED IN A CONTEMPORARY LEXICON.

THE TRADITIONAL DEN

Moving from public spaces of the home to the den, you notice the change immediately. The furnishings are more inviting and less precious; sofas and chairs are deeper, softer, and dressed in upholsteries that invite you to curl up in them. The walls change from smooth paper, drywall, or formal plaster to textured paneling or rough-hewn boards. Even the flooring is different, whether harder or softer, having an easy-to-clean, low-maintenance factor distinguishable from floors in the remainder of the home.

This is the traditional den, the original family room popularized after World War II. Generally situated in the rear of the home and adjoining the kitchen, it is the informal living space devoted to the family. Here, snacks can be nibbled without a fuss; TV, videos, and stereo can be enjoyed without worries about hiding electronics gadgetry; toddlers and pets, as a rule, can wander at ease.

In its post–World War II form, the den suggested a retreat, a place for hibernation, darker than the other living spaces of the home. Deep-stained paneling and a brick or stone fireplace were *de rigueur*, as was an overall somber palette. Today's den can still possess this dark, enveloping quality, but its definition has broadened considerably. The den in the '90s might be filled with soft lights from a bank of windows and feature whitewashed cedar paneling, a pickled oak floor, and an inviting, white-painted fireplace. The hatches no longer have to be battened; doors or windows can be flung open to the outdoors, creating a cheery, inviting effect.

Today's den may be a protected haven, an open, relaxed gathering place, or any variation thereof; what every den has in common is the feeling of home.

Left: THE BEST OF BOTH WORLDS, THIS TRADITIONAL FAMILY ROOM OFFERS THE ENVELOPING COMFORT OF THE QUINTESSENTIAL DEN, WITH ITS STONE FIREPLACE AND SOFT FURNISHINGS, AS WELL AS AN AIRIER, MORE CONTEMPORARY SENSE OF LIGHT AND SPACE, THANKS TO THE MULTITUDE OF WINDOWS, PALE PALETTE, AND HIGH CEILING.

Left: IN A LOG HOME, THE INVITING FAMILY ROOM IS A NATURAL EXTENSION OF AN ABUNDANCE OF EXISTING BUILDING MATERIALS, REQUIRING LITTLE MORE THAN TAKING ADVANTAGE OF WHAT THE HOME INHERENTLY HAS TO OFFER. CHINKED WIDE-PINE LOG WALLS AND A PALER PINE FLOOR CREATE A LODGE-LIKE WARMTH, COMPLEMENTED BY A TOWERING FIELDSTONE FIREPLACE. BOOKSHELVES, GAMEBOARDS, COMFORTABLE SEATING, AND A MIX OF ANTIQUES AND NEW FURNISHINGS ARE THE FINISHING TOUCHES.

Right: THE LONG, LEAN LINES OF A LOGGIA CREATE AN IDEAL SPACE FOR A DEN, WITH BREEZY ACCESS TO THE OUTDOORS. THIS RESTFUL ROOM FEATURES AN ECLECTIC MIX OF TRADITIONAL YET COMFORTABLE SEATING WITH CONTEMPORARY ART AND ACCESSORIES, CAPTURING THE VARIED INTERESTS OF THE OWNERS.

Above: One of the appealing qualities of the traditional den today is its ability to reflect the decorating style of the owners. Dark-paneled walls and braided rugs aren't for everyone, as this more dressed-up den illustrates. Here, taste takes a formal turn, with personality finding expression in a collection of antique blue-and-white porcelain and period antiques. Still, comfort is the key to the space, with wingback chairs providing soft spots for cozying up with a book or simply enjoying a fire.

Left: IN SOME HOMES, THE ONLY DISTINCTION BETWEEN A LIVING ROOM AND A FAMILY ROOM LIES IN THE LEVEL OF INFORMALITY AND BECKONING LIVABILITY OF THE SPACE. ANY DOUBTS ABOUT WHICH FUNCTION THIS ROOM SERVES ARE REMOVED BY THE INVITING MISSION ROCKING CHAIR AND THE INFORMAL PLACEMENT OF OTHER SEATED PIECES.

Right: EVEN A CALIFORNIA HOME IN THE CANYONS OF LOS ANGELES HAS A WARM HEART AT ITS CENTER, IN THE FORM OF A COZY FAMILY ROOM REPLETE WITH PANELED WALLS, ECLECTIC FABRICS, AND A MENAGERIE OF FAVORITE ANIMAL-THEMED ACCESSORIES. THIS SPACE LEAVES LITTLE DOUBT AS TO THE SINGULAR TASTES OF ITS OWNERS.

Above: Designed to serve the family, not to alienate it, this den incorporates an interplay of light and dark for a mood that's at once uplifting and soothing. In a surprising departure from the quintessential den, the paneling is not dark, but rather a source of light, painted a pale, creamy hue. The warmer tones emanate from the fireplace brick and the burnished palette of the upholstery. Flea-market finds give clues to the family's interests.

Above: MORE THAN ANY OTHER SPACE IN THE HOME, THE FAMILY ROOM ALLOWS THE REAL PERSONALITIES OF THE OWNERS TO SPEAK WITHOUT RESERVATION. THE OWNERS OF THIS HOME HAVE AN UNERRING EYE FOR DESIGN THAT ENABLES ELOQUENT EXPRESSION OF A RANGE OF INTERESTS, FROM CONTEMPORARY FURNISHINGS LIKE THE UNDULATING COCKTAIL TABLE AND CHROME-AND-LEATHER SEATING TO FOLK ART, LITERATURE, AND THE OCCASIONAL FUNKY FIND, CREATING A TRULY PERSONAL VERSION OF THE TRADITIONAL DEN.

Above: A CENTRAL FUNCTION OF THE DEN IS TO SOOTHE. THE IDEA OF THE DEN AS A TRANQUIL HAVEN FOR ENJOYING MORE REFLECTIVE MOMENTS IS BEAUTIFULLY CONVEYED IN THIS SERENE ROOM, IN WHICH THE WALLS, CEILING, FIREPLACE, AND FURNISHINGS ARE SO CLOSELY RELATED IN COLOR VALUE AS TO GIVE A MONOCHROMATIC IMPRESSION. THE WOVEN NAVAJO RUG, THE ONLY PATTERN IN THE ROOM, PRECLUDES THE POSSIBILITY OF ANY RESIDUAL CHILL FROM THE SUBTLE PALETTE.

Above: AS THE TRUEST MIRROR OF THE HOMEOWNER'S SELF, THE FAMILY ROOM IN THIS HOME POINTS TO A PERSONALITY THAT IS DEFINITELY MARCHING TO A DIFFERENT DRUM, WITH AN APPRECIATION FOR THE OFFBEAT AND THE UNEXPECTED. THE COMBINATIONS HERE ARE JOLTING—MASSIVE ARCHITECTURAL FEATURES TOWER OVER TINY TABLES; STYLES RANGE FROM TURN-OF-THE-CENTURY ARCHITECTURE TO 1960S FURNISHINGS. **Left:** A RICH, MASCULINE FLAVOR PERVADES THIS DEN, FROM THE PICTURE-FRAME PANELING AND BUILT-IN BOOKSHELVES TO THE VIBRANT RED LEATHER WINGBACK CHAIRS AND DEEP BLUE CURTAINS WITH RED TRIM. A SOFT THROW PILED ON THE ARM OF A CHAIR, A PLATE OF APPLES, AND A GAME OF DOMINOES PROVE THAT THE DEN, NO MATTER HOW REFINED, IS USER-FRIENDLY FOR THE ENTIRE FAMILY.

Below: THIS ROOM TAKES MAXIMUM ADVANTAGE OF THE TRADITIONAL LOCATION OF THE DEN AT THE REAR OF THE HOME. THE ENTIRE EXTERIOR WALL HAS BEEN OPENED UP WITH AN EXPANSE OF CUSTOM WINDOWS HIGH IN STYLE AND DIMENSION, ALLOWING THE ROOM TO EXTEND ONTO A DECK OVERLOOKING THE BACKYARD.

Above: WARM PLAID UPHOLSTERY FABRICS, A WOVEN INDIAN RUG, AND OTHER SOUTHWESTERN TEXTILES CREATE A VIBRANT ATMOSPHERE THAT'S CASUAL ENOUGH FOR FAMILY USE, YET SUFFICIENTLY STYLISH FOR ENTERTAINING GUESTS. THIS FAMILY ROOM EMBRACES THE CONCEPT OF THE TRADITIONAL DEN WITH ITS OLD-FASHIONED IRON STOVE, AND ENLARGES IT WITH ITS SOARING, TRUSSED PINE CEILING.

Below: A FONDNESS FOR FOLK ART, ESPECIALLY WITH A HISPANIC FLAVOR, IS CLEARLY ANNOUNCED IN THIS SMALL DEN. MUCH OF THE ROOM'S APPEAL DERIVES FROM THE UNEXPECTED MIX OF TRADITIONAL ARCHITECTURE WITH FOLKSY FURNISHINGS.

Above: A DEN IN THE HEART OF THE CITY DRAWS ITS CHARACTER FROM ITS URBAN ENVIRONS, ACHIEVING A COOL, SOPHISTICATED ELEGANCE. WISELY, THE OWNERS TURNED THE CITYSCAPE JUST OUTSIDE INTO AN INTEGRAL PART OF THE ROOM BY EMBRACING THE VIEW WITH WINDOWS LEFT COVERED ONLY BY A SHEER VALANCE, RATHER THAN CAMOUFLAGED BY A DISGUISE OF HEAVY DRAPERY.

Above: A PAIR OF DUTCH-STYLE DOORS THAT SLIDE ON A ROD, RATHER THAN OPEN AT THE HINGE, ARE THE FIRST CLUE TO THE UNUSUAL IN THIS FAMILY ROOM. DECORATIVE PAINT TREATMENTS IN A PALE GOLDEN HUE ADORN WALLS AND CEILING, SUGGESTING A PLAYFUL AMBIENCE, BUT THE FURNISHINGS THEMSELVES ARE DARK AND LEATHER, MORE TYPICAL OF THE CLASSIC DEN. THE EFFECT IS INTERESTING AND PERSONAL, DEFYING AN EASY CLASSIFICATION OF DECORATING STYLE. **Right:** DRAMATIC SHEER AUBERGINE CURTAINS ACCENTUATING THE HIGH-FLUNG TRADITIONAL ARCHITECTURE OF THIS SPACE MIGHT SIGNAL A FORMAL LIVING ROOM, RATHER THAN A FAMILY ROOM WHOSE PURPOSE IS LIFE-STYLE MORE THAN "LOOK." BUT THERE IS NO MISTAKING THIS SPACE'S DESIGNATION AS A DEN, THANKS TO THE CASUAL PLACEMENT OF FURNITURE, THE INCLUSION OF A WELL-WORN FAVORITE FAMILY CHAIR, AND THE DESIGN'S ORIENTATION AROUND THE FIREPLACE.

Below: THE IDEA THAT A DEN MUST BE A SMALL, COMPACT SPACE WITH A DARK, ENVELOPING ATMOSPHERE IS REFUTED BY THIS SPACIOUS FAMILY ROOM, IN WHICH TRUSSED CEILINGS DECLARE LOFTY SPACE OVERHEAD AND THE WHITE AND GLASS WALLS CELEBRATE AIRY OPENNESS. THERE IS NO DANGER OF THE ROOM FEELING STARK OR STERILE, HOWEVER, WITH ITS STONE FIREPLACE, RUGGED WOOD FLOORING, AND CASUAL FURNISHINGS.

Above: THE KIVA FIREPLACE AND PLASTER WALLS IN THIS ADOBE HOME PROVIDE THE DECORATIVE ORIENTATION OF THE FAMILY ROOM. WALLS ARE LEFT UNADORNED, MAKING TEXTURAL STATEMENTS IN THEMSELVES, AND WRAPAROUND MODULAR SOFA SEATING SNUGGLES UP TO THE FIREPLACE, WITH ONLY A SMALL COCKTAIL TABLE IN THE CENTER BY WAY OF ADDITIONAL FURNISHINGS.

Left: A TRUMPETBLAST OF COLOR AND MODERN ART BRINGS LIFE TO THE ELEGANT ARCHITECTURE OF THIS TRADITIONAL DEN, SOFTENING WHAT COULD HAVE BEEN AN INTIMIDATING ENVIRONMENT. ALTHOUGH THE ROOM EXUDES PEDIGREE, NOT ONLY FROM ITS RICHLY DETAILED PANELING BUT ALSO DUE TO THE CALIBER OF ITS CONTEMPORARY ART AND FURNISHINGS, IT NONETHELESS HAS ALL THE INVITING ALLURE OF A CLASSIC DEN: SEATING IS CAPACIOUS AND COMFORTABLE, WELL PLACED FOR THE ENJOYMENT OF CONVERSATION AND A CRACKLING FIRE.

Below: WITH THE FIREPLACE AS ITS FOCAL POINT, THIS DEN ENSURES ENJOYMENT OF THE HEARTH WITH A FURNITURE ARRANGEMENT THAT POSITIONS A PAIR OF COMFORTABLE WINGBACK CHAIRS AT FIRESIDE, WITH A FUNCTIONAL TABLE IN BETWEEN. CHAIR FABRICS ARE IN THE SAME COLOR FAMILY BUT IN TWO DISTINCTIVE PATTERNS, ENHANCING THE FEELING OF UNSTUDIED STYLE.

Above: AN ANTIQUE HOME PRESENTS A UNIQUE OPPORTUNITY FOR DESIGNING A FAMILY ROOM THAT BESPEAKS A HOMEY, PERSONAL CHARM. THE ORIGINAL HEADBOARD CEILING, ALONG WITH EXPOSED HEWN BEAMS, WAS RETAINED IN THIS SPACE TO CREATE AMBIENCE OVERHEAD, WITH A HANGING DISPLAY OF DRIED HERBS AND ANTIQUE BASKETS. A BRAIDED RUG, YESTERYEAR FABRIC PATTERNS, FOLK ART, AND ANTIQUE ACCESSORIES AND FURNISHINGS REINFORCE THE OLD-STYLE WARMTH OF THE ARCHITECTURE WHILE AT THE SAME TIME EXPRESSING THE FAMILY'S INTERESTS.

Above: DESPITE ITS RELATIVELY SMALL SPACE, THIS DEN PROJECTS WARMTH AND

A SINGULAR ROBUST FLAIR DUE, IN LARGE PART, TO THE SELECTION OF RED AS THE

DOMINANT COLOR. REPEATED ON FURNITURE COVERINGS, OTHER TEXTILES, AND A VIBRANT

LAMP SHADE, THE BOLD RED HUE DRAWS THE ROOM TOGETHER, SURPRISINGLY ENHANCING

RATHER THAN REDUCING ITS SENSE OF SPACIOUSNESS.

Above: IN A CONTEMPORARY HOME, THE FAMILY ROOM DOESN'T HAVE TO BE AN AFTERTHOUGHT, A TACKED-ON HOMAGE TO TRADITIONAL DESIGN. INSTEAD, AS EVIDENCED BY THIS SPACE, IT CAN BE AN INHERENT PART OF THE ARCHITECTURE. BUILT-IN BANQUETTE SEATING CIRCUMSCRIBES THE FIREPLACE, WHILE THE DEN ITSELF IS SUNKEN, DESCENDING FROM A SMALL ATRIUM—ALL PART OF THE ORIGINAL ARCHITECTURAL DESIGN. **Left:** THIS CLASSIC DEN, WITH ITS DARK PANELED WALLS AND FIREPLACE, ESCHEWS A DATED LOOK BY INCORPORATING FURNISHINGS THAT ARTICULATE COLOR BLOCKS—ONE OF DECORATING'S NEWEST LOOKS.

Above: As one of the most personal spaces in the home, the family room presents an opportunity to engage in wish-fulfillment.
This home's ranch-style architecture is a launching pad for realizing the Wild West fantasy. The western theme pervades the space
through bronzes, covered-wagon accessories and art, wagon-wheel furniture, and Indian rugs.

Left: THE SERENE, SETTLED AMBIENCE OF A GRACIOUS LIBRARY OR STUDY CHARACTERIZES THIS DEN. BOOKS LINE THE WALLS FOR LAZY PERUSAL, WHILE A WET BAR FACILITATES A DIFFERENT SORT OF AFTER-DINNER RELAXATION. ENJOYMENT OF THE BLAZING FIRE IS ENCOURAGED BY THE PRESENCE OF PLUSH CHAIRS AND A PLUMP SOFA.

Right: BEAUTIFULLY BALANCED WITH ITS SYMMETRICALLY PLACED WINDOWS AND FURNISHINGS, THIS DEN IS THE BEST OF BOTH WORLDS: LIGHT AND AIRY, YET AT THE SAME TIME COZY AND COMFORTING. THE DESIGN IS INFORMAL YET TRADITIONAL, WITH SUBTLE OVERTONES OF COUNTRY.

The Great Room

With its open spaces that serve a multitude of needs, the great room caters to the way families live today. Like the colonial era's keeping room, the great room often features a fireplace and seating area, plus a dining table, accommodating the functions of everyday living and eating, which so often overlap. This room not only serves the needs of the family, but is also an ideal space for entertaining. Cozy seating areas facilitate conversations, while a dining table placed in the same room means that hors d'oeuvres may be enjoyed without having to move from room to room. The wide walls of the great room afford ample space for freestanding entertainment units or built-in shelving to house home electronics equipment. With its multipurpose functions, the great room promises to be the most lived-in space in the modern home.

The great room lends itself to almost any architectural style, from early primitive to contemporary high-tech. Typically, the ceiling of the great room is lofty, enhancing the already capacious sense of space. In a rustic, country-style home, the great room's ceiling might feature old salvaged hand-hewn beams that are left exposed for rugged, vintage interest. In a contemporary home, the ceiling of the great room might be vaulted and painted a pristine white, emphasizing spare lines and form more than texture or ornamentation.

Like the den, the great room is usually situated at the rear of the house, either opening onto or facing the grounds behind the home. It is not uncommon for the room to capitalize on its large scale by embracing panoramic views through broad expanses of glass. Such wide, high windows make the room one of the brightest and lightest in the house, in contrast to the traditional den, which tends to be a bit more enclosed and enveloping.

No matter whether it is furnished in a spare, stream-lined fashion or a cozy, old-fashioned country style, the great room is perfect for the modern family life-style.

Left: As life-styles change, the function of the family room changes, too. In many homes, a great room, which has more space to house electronic entertainment equipment, is the preferred choice over the smaller, traditional den. Here, the brick fireplace incorporates an electronics niche.

Above: A STEP-UP KITCHEN OPENS ONTO THIS SUNKEN FAMILY ROOM, CREATING

A CASUAL ATMOSPHERE WITH A CONVENIENT, PRACTICAL FUNCTION: THE HOST OR HOSTESS

NEED NOT DISAPPEAR INTO THE KITCHEN FOR FINAL MEAL PREPARATIONS, BUT CAN EASILY

COMMUNE WITH GUESTS OR FAMILY MEMBERS SEATED JUST BELOW.

Left: THE GREAT ROOM, ONE OF THE MOST POPULAR FORMS OF FAMILY ROOM IN TODAY'S HOMES, IS BY DEFINITION OPEN AND SPACIOUS. IN THIS HOME, PERIOD ARCHITECTURE AND COUNTRY STYLE COMBINE WITH A MODERN SENSIBILITY—ONLY A COUNTER WORK SPACE DIVIDES THE KITCHEN FROM THE LARGER EXPANSE OF FAMILY ROOM—AND EVEN THE COUNTER IS OPEN AT THE TOP, SANS CUPBOARDS.

Right: THIS GREAT ROOM DIVIDES ITS FUNCTIONS INTO TWO DISTINCT AREAS: A SNUG SPACE FOR READING OR VISITING WITH FAMILY AND FRIENDS ON COMFORTABLE CHAIRS AND SOFAS, AND A SMALL DINING AREA FOR TAKING AN INFORMAL MEAL OR A CUP OF COFFEE. THE KITCHEN OPENS ONTO THE DINING AREA, ALLOWING FAMILY MEMBERS TO MOVE EASILY FROM COOKING TO DINING TO SOCIALIZING.

Above: THIS GREAT ROOM COMBINES DIVERSE FEATURES TO CUSTOM-FIT ITS OWNERS. THE LOW-SLUNG ARCHITECTURE WITH ITS RECESSED LIGHTING AND EXPANSES OF GLASS IS CONTEMPORARY, WHILE THE FIREPLACE MANTEL IS TRADITIONAL. ANTIQUES ADD A RUGGED PRESENCE TO THE CLEAN, NEUTRAL PALETTE.

Above: DECKED IN SLICK WHITE, WITH LINEAR CONTEMPORARY WINDOWS, SKYLIGHTS, AND HIGH-TECH BLACK ACCENTS, THIS FAMILY ROOM PUTS A FRESH SPIN ON THE IDEA OF COZY. THE MODULAR SEATING IS COMFORTABLE AND BECKONING, INVITING FAMILY MEMBERS AND FRIENDS TO RELAX BEFORE THE FIRE. INTERESTINGLY, THIS SPACE IS DEVOID OF ANY OF THE BRIC-A-BRAC OR HOMEY ACCESSORIES THAT TYPICALLY CHARACTERIZE A FAMILY ROOM, WITH THE RESULT THAT FAMILY MEMBERS ARE ENCOURAGED TO CONCENTRATE ON EACH OTHER.

Above: MORE THAN THE PUBLIC SPACES IN THE HOME, THE FAMILY ROOM REPRESENTS AN OPPORTUNITY TO REVEAL THE UNIQUE PERSONALITIES AND PREDILECTIONS OF THE HOME OWNERS. THIS GREAT ROOM HAS A HIGH-STYLE DESIGN THAT REFLECTS THE ONE-OF-A-KIND AESTHETIC TASTES OF ITS OWNERS. THE ELEPHANT-PATTERNED BATIK FABRIC ON THE SOFA AND ABOVE THE DOORWAY COMBINE WITH THE ZEBRA-STRIPED RUG IN THE DINING ALCOVE TO IMPART AN ETHNIC FLAVOR TO THE ROOM, WHILE FAVORITE *OBJETS D'ART* DISPLAYED ON VERTICAL SHELVING ADD A PERSONAL TOUCH.

Below: THIS CONTEMPORARY BEACHFRONT GREAT ROOM COMBINES PERIOD

FURNITURE, COLLECTIBLES, AND ART FOR A SUNNY UPDATE

OF THE EIGHTEENTH-CENTURY KEEPING ROOM.

Above: ANY NOTIONS THAT A FAMILY ROOM AND STELLAR

STYLE ARE MUTUALLY EXCLUSIVE TERMS STOPS HERE. THE GRAND,

CONTEMPORARY ARCHITECTURE OF THIS GREAT ROOM, WITH ITS

SOARING CEILINGS AND BOLD GEOMETRY MAKES A FAMILY GATHERING

AN AESTHETIC EXPERIENCE OF THE HIGHEST ORDER.

Above: THE GREAT ROOM DOESN'T HAVE TO ENCOMPASS AN ENORMOUS AREA TO GET

THE JOB DONE. ALL THE NECESSARY INGREDIENTS—A FIREPLACE, COMFORTABLE SEATING, AND A

DINING TABLE—ARE PRESENT IN THIS MODERATELY SIZED SPACE.

Left: A CHEF'S DREAM, THIS GREAT ROOM ALLOWS CULINARY DUTIES TO BE PERFORMED WITHOUT A PAUSE IN CONVERSATION. THE KITCHEN WORK COUNTER (VISIBLE IN THE FOREFRONT OF THE PHOTO) OVERLOOKS THE FAMILY ROOM'S DINING SPACE AND SEATING AREA, PROVING THE MERITS OF A MULTIFUNCTIONAL ROOM DESIGN.

Right: AN INFORMAL, INDIGENOUS ARCHITECTURAL STYLE REMINISCENT OF THE WORK OF FRANK LLOYD WRIGHT CREATES AN APPROPRIATELY WARM ATMOSPHERE FOR A GREAT ROOM. THE DINING CHAIRS AND WOOD FLOORING COMPLEMENT THE ARCHITECTURE, CREATING AN INVITING SPACE THAT ISN'T RELIANT ON ADDITIONAL DECORATIVE OBJECTS FOR ITS COMPELLING AMBIENCE.

Above: Taking an L-shape from the outline of the kitchen,

this great room provides two discrete areas—one for conversation in front

of the fireplace, another for casual dining in front of the windows, with no

visual barriers in between. The curvaceous shapes and deep colors in the seating

area make it a warm and inviting corner.

Above: A FAMILY ROOM CAN BE CREATED FROM VIRTUALLY ANY EXISTING SPACE IN THE HOME.

HERE, A SOLARIUM SERVES THE FUNCTION OF A GREAT ROOM, COMPLETE WITH AN INTIMATE SEATING AREA BEFORE THE

FIREPLACE, ELECTRONIC ENTERTAINMENT EQUIPMENT STORED IN A CONSOLE, AND A CASUAL DINING AREA.

WITH THE GLASS WALLS AND CEILING, THE ROOM IS AS AIRY AS THE OUTDOORS ITSELF.

Right: SATURATED IN JEWEL-TONE COLORS AND FUNKY COWBOY CHARM, THIS GREAT ROOM IS WHERE THE OLD WEST MEETS CREATURE COMFORTS HEAD-ON, WITH SOME LIVELY, FUN RESULTS. **Below:** DESPITE ITS STREAMLINED CONTEMPORARY STYLE, THIS FAMILY ROOM HAS ITS ORIGINS IN COLONIAL TIMES, IN THE KEEPING ROOM THAT INCORPORATED A SEATING AREA FOR FAMILY WITHIN CLOSE PROXIMITY TO THE KITCHEN FIREPLACE. NO FIREPLACE GRACES THIS ROOM, BUT ITS OPEN FLOW INTO THE KITCHEN NONETHELESS ECHOES THE IDEA OF THE ERSTWHILE KEEPING ROOM.

Just For Fun

Among the types of family rooms, the media rooms and play or recreation rooms offer the greatest flexibility in terms of architecture and location within the home. Almost any room in the house, including a spare guest room or an open room in the basement, can suffice. Rather than operating as a general-purpose hangout, this family room is geared specifically to entertainment.

As a media room (or TV room, as it was known before home electronics became increasingly sophisticated, affordable, and available), all the space really needs is adequate room for setting up equipment and providing comfortable seating. This makes the media room an attractive option as a family room in a home whose floor plan includes only one living space: A bedroom, study, unused garage, or any other spare space, regardless of its architectural interest (or lack thereof), may be easily converted to serve this purpose. A fireplace is a luxury, not a staple, as are a view and space for a dining table. It makes no difference whether the media room opens into the kitchen or onto the backyard. No wonder many families find the media room a convenient solution for freeing up a single living room from potentially space-stealing and visually obtrusive TV and stereo equipment.

Similarly, the play or recreation room has no etched-in-stone standards of form. In regions of the country in which houses include basements, the play room often is relegated to this lower level. And for practical reasons: The basement serves as a noise shield for the remainder of the home, and it can have a lower-maintenance, less-finished appearance that better suits the play function. Parents appreciate the virtues of a rec room designated especially for children: Toys, noise, and playmates can be indulged freely, without disrupting the more organized life-style of the adults. Of course, the rec room can also serve as a playground for adults. Pool tables, dart boards, game tables, TVs, stereos, and displays of sporting equipment find a comfortable home here, which might be awkward or impossible in more integrated living spaces of the home.

Left: ONE FORM OF FAMILY ROOM HINGES ON THE PHILOSOPHY OF SHEER FUN. THIS EXUBERANT SPACE COMES TO LIFE WITH A COLORFUL COLLECTION OF 1950S AND '60S TOYS, FURNITURE, BUTTONS, AND OTHER COLLECTIBLES. THE FUN TELEVISION, GUITAR, AND MAP FIT SNUGLY INTO A DESIGN THAT HAPPILY PLEADS A CASE FOR PLAY.

Right: A MORE REFINED FAMILY ROOM DEVOTED TO PLAY AND OTHER PERSONAL PURSUITS HAS A CLEAN, NO-CLUTTER LOOK WITH SNOW-WHITE WALLS AND FURNISHINGS. BUT WITH A GAME TABLE AT ITS CENTER AND BUILT-IN BOOKSHELVES AT ITS FLANKS, THE ROOM CLEARLY IS DESIGNED WITH FUNCTION IN MIND. **Below:** A HIGH-GLOSS MEDIA ROOM THAT IS A SALIENT STATEMENT OF CONTEMPORARY DESIGN IS AN APPROPRIATE BACKDROP FOR THE SOPHISTICATED ELECTRONIC ENTERTAINMENT EQUIPMENT IT HOUSES. BLACK LACQUERED SHELVING HOLDS A COLLECTION OF PERIOD ENTERTAINMENT COLLECTIBLES, PROVIDING AN IRONIC COUNTERPOINT TO THE ROOM'S STATE-OF-THE-ART, HIGH-TECH FEEL.

Right: IN A DEPARTURE FROM THE TYPICAL FAMILY REC ROOM, WHICH OFTEN FEATURES CUSHIONY FURNITURE THAT INVITES SPRAWLING UPON, THIS GRAPHIC SPACE, WITH ITS SQUARE MOTIFS IN WOOD, HOSTS COLORFUL CHAIRS, BARSTOOLS, AND A TABLE AS THE MOST FUNCTIONAL MEANS TO AN END. THE TABLE AND BAR CAN SERVE AS SURFACES FOR INFORMAL MEALS OR GAMES, WHILE THE CHAIRS PROVIDE SEATS AS VANTAGE POINTS FOR WATCHING TELEVISION, FOR CONVERSATION, OR FOR READING.

Above: Strictly for kids, this family play room is every child's fantasy. With hot-air

balloons soaring across the walls and primary-colored banquette seating,

the multifarious space is a stimulating environment for development through play.

Left: THIS FAMILY ROOM IN THE CITY IS A COMPATIBLE EXTEN-
SION OF THE VIEWS IT EMBRACES THROUGH LARGE, PLATE-GLASS
WINDOWS. QUIETLY SOPHISTICATED WITH A NO-PATTERN, NEUTRAL
PALETTE THAT INCLUDES A SMATTERING OF CHIC BLACK LEATHER, IT IS
AN ABOVE-IT-ALL RETREAT FOR WATCHING TELEVISION OR ENJOYING
A DRINK FROM ITS HIGH-RISE VANTAGE POINT.

Right: THIS RECREATION ROOM EMBRACES THE
CAREFREE JOYS OF CHILDHOOD WITH A BOLDLY
COLORED DESIGN AND LOFTY CONTEMPORARY
ARCHITECTURE ANY ADULT CAN APPRECIATE.
THE RED AND YELLOW PALETTE ESTABLISHED IN
THE FURNISHINGS EXTENDS TO THE ARCHITECTURE,
AS SEEN IN THE BRILLIANT, DIAGONAL STRIPES ON
A FREESTANDING ARCHITECTURAL ARMOIRE AND THE
WOOD TRIM AND ROLL-UP SHADES ON
THE WINDOWS.

Above: Furniture manufacturers have rallied to the market demand for quality casegoods to house sophisticated media-room electronics. All of the family's home entertainment equipment can be housed in this single piece, facilitating the uncluttered design that characterizes the spare yet cozy family room.

Above: WITH ADEQUATE PLANNING AND A LITTLE INGENUITY, BEAUTIFUL TRADITIONAL ARCHITECTURE CAN PLAY HOST TO HOME ELECTRONICS IN A FAMILY ROOM THAT PROVES MODERN-DAY PASTIMES CAN PEACEFULLY COEXIST WITH THE MOST GRACEFUL OF INTERIORS.

Above: PLANNING IS THE KEY TO THE SUCCESS OF THIS ELEGANT, DELICIOUSLY SIMPLE CONTEMPORARY FAMILY ROOM THAT SERVES THE OWNERS' HOME-MEDIA NEEDS. STRIPPED OF SUPERFLUOUS HARDWARE, A WALL OF BUILT-IN SHELVING AND CABINETRY THAT ALSO HOUSES A LARGE-SCREEN TELEVISION, STEREO COMPONENTS, AND A BAR GIVES THE SPACE ITS STREAMLINED LOOK.

Above: HIGH TECH'S COLD EDGE MELTS AWAY IN THIS WARM FAMILY ROOM, THANKS TO THE TERRA-COTTA TILE FLOOR,

BECKONING SEATING, AND THE FAMILY'S READING MATERIALS AND TROPHIES ON A WALL OF BUILT-IN BOOKSHELVES.

STILL, THE AUDIO EQUIPMENT THAT IS HOUSED IN A FLOOR-TO-CEILING CUSTOM WALL UNIT IS STATE OF-THE-ART.

Below: HOME ELECTRONICS ARE AN INSTITUTION OF TODAY'S FAMILY LIFE AND, THEREFORE, A PRIMARY FEATURE OF TODAY'S FAMILY ROOMS. THIS SOPHISTICATED DEN TAKES THE CHILL OFF ELECTRONICS EQUIPMENT BY CONTAINING IT WITHIN A WARM WOOD ANTIQUE ARMOIRE. WHEN NOT ACTIVELY ENGAGED, THE TELEVISION CAN DISAPPEAR BEHIND CLOSED DOORS.

Above: EVEN IF THE FAMILY'S ENTERTAINMENT NEEDS ARE IN CONFLICT WITH THEIR DECORATING GOALS, WITH A LITTLE CREATIVITY, A HAPPY SOLUTION CAN STILL BE ATTAINED. HERE, THE SOFT WHITE THEME OF THE FAMILY ROOM REIGNS SUPREME, AS A RESULT OF WHITE FOLDING DOORS THAT, WHEN CLOSED, GIVE THE ROOM A UNIFIED, SERENE LOOK, YET WHEN OPEN, ALLOW THE TELEVISION AND BAR TO BE ENJOYED.

Above: WHEN THE TELEVISION AND STEREO ARE FREQUENTLY EMPLOYED, IT MAKES PERFECT

SENSE TO INTEGRATE THEM INTO THE DESIGN OF THE FAMILY ROOM. IN THIS GRACEFUL SPACE, THE

UTILITARIAN ELECTRONICS BLEND INTO THE DECOR AS PART OF BUILT-IN SHELVING THAT ALSO DISPLAYS

BOOKS AND COLLECTIBLES.

Above: EVEN IF SPACE IS AT A PREMIUM, THE FAMILY ROOM CAN SERVE A MULTITUDE OF FUNCTIONS IF INNOVATIVELY DESIGNED. A TELEVISION

AND STEREO EQUIPMENT OCCUPY MINIMAL SPACE AND PRESENT MINIMAL VISUAL OBSTRUCTION IN THIS SMALL FAMILY ROOM AS A RESULT OF A

NARROW STRIP OF BUILT-IN SHELVING THAT EXTENDS ALMOST TO THE CEILING. THE ROOM RETAINS A SYMMETRICAL BALANCE BECAUSE THE SHELVING'S

HEIGHT, WIDTH, AND MOLDING IDENTICALLY MATCH THAT OF THE DOOR ON THE OPPOSITE SIDE OF THE FIREPLACE. **Right:** KNOTTY-PINE WALLS

AND CEILING AND A STRATEGICALLY PLACED SKYLIGHT LEND A LODGE LOOK TO THIS REC ROOM. THE POOL TABLE IS THE FOCAL POINT, BUT BANQUETTE

SEATING AROUND THE ROOM'S PERIMETER ALLOWS FOR LOUNGING WITH A BOOK OR JUST PASSING TIME. A SPORTS THEME IS ARTICULATED WITH

WALL ART, WHICH INCLUDES FAMILY SPORTS PHOTOS, AWARDS, AND TROPHIES.

PERSONAL PROFILE

In all its variations, the family room reflects the interior portrait—the true self—of the family that occupies it. The impersonal facade of the home's public spaces stops here. Family rooms express the identity and interests of the family through collectibles that the family truly loves—objects that tell more than show; through family photos that might clutter or disrupt the design of a more formal living space; through family heirlooms such as a grandmother's wedding dress, shadow-boxed and hung on the wall; or through musical instruments and favorite books—including paperbacks, not just coffee-table curiosities.

The family room isn't about impressing but rather, expressing. As the heart of the home, the family room has an obligation to project a sense of safety, security, and comfort. Its first call to duty is to be entirely livable. There's no room for anything too precious here. Comfortable seating is essential—big, overstuffed sectionals, sofas, and chairs; recliners; and rocking chairs that really work. Patterns and textures should invite use, rather than prohibit it. Nothing is too fussy or incompatible with wear or spills.

For all its comfort and low maintenance, the family room is anything but dull. In the home's interior design, this room can be the most audacious, featuring brighter colors than are found in more formal spaces. It even can be designed in a totally different style—such as cowboy or lodge—that would be inappropriate for the entire home. It is rich in textural interest, from rough, pickled cedar siding to ripply Saltillo tiles or lumpy wool Berber carpeting.

The family room is about how you live, but it's also about who you are.

Above: FURNITURE ARRANGEMENT BISECTS THIS FAMILY ROOM INTO A LIBRARY AREA AND A CONVERSATION AREA, WITHOUT THE AID OF ARCHITECTURE.

Left: A SENSE OF YESTERYEAR ADDS HOMEY COMFORT TO THIS FAMILY ROOM THROUGH ANTIQUE ROCKING HORSES AND OTHER OLD COLLECTIBLES.

THE WHITE UPHOLSTERY FABRICS AND TABLE SKIRT PREVENT THE SPACE FROM BECOMING BUSY, SERVING AS "AIR" AGAINST THE RICH, PATTERNED RUG.

Left: ONE FAMILY'S DESIRE TO BRING RUSTIC, OUTDOOR WARMTH TO THE PLAIN WHITE ARCHITECTURE OF ITS FAMILY ROOM IS BEAUTIFULLY EXECUTED IN THIS SMALL SPACE, WITH ITS RICH TEXTURE, COLOR, AND "FOUND" ACCESSORIES. ADDING ARCHITECTURE WHERE THERE IS NONE IS A ROW OF TALL TWIG BRANCHES RISING UP BEHIND THE SOFA. RATTAN AND IRON FURNISHINGS, A TWIG BASKET, A WOVEN FISHING CREEL, DRIED FLOWERS, AND FOLK-ART FISH DECOYS COMPLETE THE ONE-OF-A-KIND LOOK.

Right: WITH A FEW OUTSTANDING PIECES OF ART AND FURNITURE, A FAMILY ROOM CAN RETAIN A CALMING AMBIENCE AND STILL PROJECT THE PERSONALITIES OF THOSE WHO LIVE WITHIN IT. THIS ROOM HINGES ON THE PAINTING AND COFFEE TABLE, WITH THE REMAINDER OF THE DECOR REINFORCING THE IMPORTANCE OF THOSE PIECES.

Right: THIS FAMILY ROOM PROJECTS ITS OWNERS' PERSONALITIES AT A GLANCE. THE PLATE COLLECTION SPANS THE FULL WIDTH OF TWO SHELVES AT THE CEILING, FRAMING, ALONG WITH SHELVES OF BOOKS, AN ART COLLECTION IN THE CENTER OF THE WALL. THE VIBRANT RED PALETTE PROVIDES A STIMULATING ATMOSPHERE, ACTUALLY INCREASING THE ADRENALIN OF THOSE WITHIN THE ROOM.

Left: ESSENTIALLY ARCHITECTURAL IN CHARACTER, THIS FAMILY ROOM WITTILY ESTABLISHES THE OWNER'S PASSION FOR THE CLASSICS. FROM THE CHAUCERIAN LINES STENCILED AROUND THE PERIMETER TO THE CUSTOM-DESIGNED NEOCLASSICAL BOOKSHELVES, THIS ROOM'S DESIGN IS A LIGHTHEARTED EXPRESSION OF A FAMILY'S LOVE OF LITERATURE.

Below: CONTEMPORARY ARCHITECTURE AND FURNISHINGS MERGE WITH PRIMITIVE COLLECTIBLES IN THIS FAMILY ROOM TO EXPRESS THE RANGE OF ITS OWNERS' INTERESTS.

Above: THE FAMILY ROOM CAN BE A SHOWCASE FOR DISPLAYING ANY ARRAY OF OBJECTS THAT HAVE SPECIAL MEANING FOR THE HOME OWNERS. THESE MINIATURE CHINA CUPS AND SAUCERS ARE THE RESULT OF YEARS OF COLLECTING. ARTFULLY PRESENTED ON ANTIQUE SHELVES INSET IN BARNBOARD PANELING, THE DISPLAY EXPRESSES A SINGULAR STYLE. **Left:** WHEN READING IS THE FAMILY PASSION, THE FAMILY ROOM BECOMES A REPOSITORY FOR THAT FAVORITE RECREATION. IN LIBRARY FASHION, SHELVES TOWER UP THE ELONGATED WINDOWS OF THIS FAMILY ROOM, MERITING A LADDER AND A SMALL LIBRARY TABLE FOR THOROUGH CONSUMPTION.

Right: MORE THAN AN ASSEMBLAGE OF FURNITURE AND ACCESSORIES, THIS FAMILY ROOM REVEALS ITS OWNERS' ATTENTION TO PLANNING AND DETAIL WITH A SERIES OF BUILT-IN, CANTILEVERED FLOOR-TO-CEILING CABINETS WITH PANELS DECORATED WITH ABSTRACT CUTOUTS REMINISCENT OF MATISSE. THE TWO FAR CUPBOARDS FEATURE OPEN SHELVING AT THE TOP FOR DISPLAYING BOOKS AND COLLECTIBLES, WHILE THE CLOSED CENTER CABINET HOUSES ELECTRONICS EQUIPMENT.

Left: THE MORE DIVERSE THE INTERESTS AND TRAVELS OF THE HOME OWNERS, THE MORE PERSONAL AND INTERESTING THE FAMILY ROOM. ORGANIZATION IS THE KEY TO SUCCESS IN AMASSING SO MANY DIVERGENT OBJECTS IN A SINGLE SPACE: ADEQUATE SHELVING ALLOWS A SINGLE, HUGE DISPLAY, WITH THE OBJECTS THEMSELVES ARRANGED LIKE A STILL LIFE WITH ATTENTION TO BALANCE AND SCALE.

Above: A LEADED GLASS WINDOW BEARING A COAT OF ARMS IS THE FIRST SIGN OF THE PERSONAL TOUCH THAT

GIVES THIS FAMILY ROOM ITS UNIQUE CHARACTER. A COLLECTION OF PHOTOGRAPHS IN CONTEMPORARY BLACK FRAMES PROPPED AGAINST

THE WALL AND UPON THE FLOOR MANIFESTS A CASUAL SPIRIT.

Left: WHEN THE PARTICULAR FORM OF THE FAMILY ROOM IS A GREAT ROOM, THE CAPACIOUS SQUARE FOOTAGE AND VOLUMINOUS VERTICAL SPACE OF THAT TERRITORY PRESENT A UNIQUE OPPORTUNITY TO PACK A MULTITUDE OF PERSONALITY INTO A SINGLE SPACE. IN ADDITION TO THE TELLING PIECES THAT FURNISH THE ROOM AND DECORATE THE WALLS, THIS SPACE'S NARRATIVE EVEN EXTENDS TO THE CEILING, WHERE AN UPTURNED CANOE TELLS A STORY OF THE GREAT OUTDOORS. **Below:** A PENCHANT FOR SCULPTURE, FOLK ART, AND BOOKS, AS WELL AS A SENSE OF THE MACABRE (AS ILLUSTRATED BY THE SKELETON SCULPTURE), ARE ALL REFLECTED IN THIS UNIQUE FAMILY ROOM THAT BRILLIANTLY BREAKS THE COOKIE-CUTTER MOLD OF FORMULAIC DECORATING.

Above: EVERY ELEMENT IN THIS FAMILY ROOM, FROM THE RICHLY PATTERNED PILLOWS AND UPHOLSTERY FABRICS TO THE GEOMETRIC-PATTERNED FLOORING AND FLAG COFFEE TABLE, MAKES A BOLD STATEMENT IN DEFENSE OF HIGH VISIBILITY. WITH ITS HISTORICAL TOUCHES, PLATES CROWNING THE DOOR-WAY, AND FISH PRINTS DRAWING THE EYE UP TO THE CEILING, THE ROOM PROJECTS VITALITY AND PERSONALITY.

SOURCES

Interior Designers

(pages 2 and 35, left)
Beverly Ellsley Interiors
Westport, CT
(203) 227-1157

(page 6)
Brian Murphy
Santa Monica, CA
(310) 459-0955

(page 10)
Mark Hutker & Associates
Vineyard Haven, MA
(508) 693-3340

(pages 12, top and 20, left)
Lyn Peterson
Motif Designs
New Rochelle, NY
(914) 633-1170

(pages 12, bottom and 13)
Charles Riley
New York, NY
(212) 206-8395

(page 14, bottom)
Debra Jones
Los Angeles, CA
(310) 476-1824

(pages 16 and 66, top)
Gary Wolf Architects, Inc.
Boston, MA
(617) 742-7557

(page 17)
Owen & Mandolfo, Architects
New York, NY
(212) 686-4576

(pages 19 and 67)
David Livingston Interiors
San Francisco, CA
(415) 392-2465

(page 20, right)
Carole and Marc Moscowitz
Design
Sherman, CT
(203) 355-2500

(page 22)
Stephen Mallory & Associates
New York, NY
(212) 737-7171

(page 23)
C & J Katz Studio
Boston, MA
(617) 367-0537

(page 24)
Jacques Grange
Paris, France
47.42.47.34

(page 25, left)
Marge Young
Marge Young Interiors
East Northport, NY
(516) 368-5150

(page 26, right)
Ronald Bricke
Ronald Bricke & Associates
New York, NY
(212) 472-9006

(page 27)
Barbara Barry
Los Angeles, CA
(310) 276-9977

(page 28)
Roy McMakin
Seattle, WA
(206) 323-6992

(page 29)
Sandra Nunnerly
New York, NY
(212) 472-9341

(page 31, top)
Diane Chapman
San Francisco, CA
(415) 346-2373

(page 31, bottom)
Ken Kelleher
Boston, MA
(617) 262-2060

(page 34)
Bettina Calderone Design
Sherman, CT
(203) 355-1995

(page 35, right)
Joe Ruggiero
Encino, CA
(818) 783-9256

(page 36)
Connie Beale
Connie Beale Interior Design
Greenwich, CT
(203) 629-3442

(pages 37 and 56, right)
Bruce Bierman
New York, NY
(212) 243-1935

(page 38)
Florence Karasik
Shrewsbury, NJ
(908) 219-8700

(pages 39, left and 41, top)
Steven Ehrlich, Architect
Venice, CA
(310) 399-7711

(page 39, right)
Al Devido
New York, NY
(212) 517-6100

(pages 41, top and 65, right)
Anita Calero
New York, NY
(212) 727-8949

(page 41, bottom)
Lori Margolis
Commercial Design Group
Summit, NJ
(908) 277-2880

(page 42)
Ron Erenberg
Santa Monica, CA
(310) 459-1515

(page 43)
Jack Lowery & Associates, Inc.
New York, NY
(212) 734-1680

(page 44)
Cathleen Schmidtknecht
Oakland, CA
(510) 339-3397

(page 45)
Janet Lohman
Los Angeles, CA
(310) 471-3955

(page 46)
Allee Willis
Los Angeles, CA
(818) 985-6317

(page 48, bottom)
Vogue Furniture
Livonia, MI
(313) 422-3890

(page 49)
Peter Lawton
Design PLUS
Shrewsbury, MA
(508) 793-9670

(page 50)
Bonnie Siracusa
Great Neck, NY
(516) 482-3349

(page 51, top)
Nicholas Calder
Nicholas Calder Interior
New York, NY
(212) 861-9055

(page 51, bottom)
Barbara Ostrom
Barbara Ostrom Associates
Mahwah, NJ
(201) 529-0444

(page 52)
Schweitzer BIM
Los Angeles, CA
(213) 936-6163

(page 54)
Ed Cohen, ISID
Edward Cohen, Inc.
New York, NY
(212) 371-1554

James Justice, ISID
Beverly Hills, CA
(310) 285-0833

(page 56, left)
Ron Meyers
Los Angeles, CA
(213) 851-7576

(page 57)
Michael De Santis
Michael De Santis, Inc.
New York, NY
(212) 753-8871

(page 58)
David Rockwell and Jay
Haverson
(formerly of Haverson/Rockwell
Architects)
New York, NY
(212) 889-4182

(page 59)
JoAnne M. Kuehner
Naples, FL
(813) 434-6001

(page 60)
Thomas F. Kenney, ASID
Saffron House Inc.
Boston, MA
(617) 737-8150

(page 61)
Nancy Mannucci, ASID
New York, NY
(212) 427-9868

(page 62, top)
Pereaux
Morristown, NJ
(201) 993-8255

(page 62, bottom)
Nancy Serafini
Homeworks
Wellesley, MA
(617) 237-7666

(page 63, top)
Carleton Varney
Dorothy Draper & Co., Inc.
New York, NY
(212) 758-2810

(page 63, bottom)
Arnelle Kase
Barbara Scavullo Design
San Francisco, CA
(415) 558-8774

(page 64)
Hugh Newell Jacobsen, FAI
Washington, D.C.
(202) 337-5200

(page 65, left)
Burr & McCallum Architects
Williamstown, MA
(413) 458-2121

(page 69, right)
Robert DeCarlo
New York, NY
(212) 245-2968

Photography credits

© Peter Aaron/Esto Photographics: p. 25 right
© Balthazar Korab: pp. 48 bottom, 64
© Grey Crawford: pp. 39 left, 41 top, 42, 69 left
© Mark Darley/Esto Photographics: p. 21 right
© Derrick & Love: pp. 22, 43
© Daniel Eifert: p. 54
© Phillip H. Ennis: pp. 24, 25 left, 26 right, 36, 40, 51 top &
bottom, 55, 57, 62 top & bottom, 69 right
© Feliciano: pp. 12 top, 20 left, 63 top
© Scott Frances/Esto Photographics: pp. 17, 65 left
© Michael Garland: pp. 14 top, 35 bottom
© Tria Giovan: pp. 12 bottom, 13, 21 left, 48 top, 56 right, 65 right
© Nancy Hill: p. 66 bottom
© Image/Dennis Krukowski: pp. 59, 61

© Tim Lee: pp. 20 right, 34
© Jennifer Levy: pp. 29, 37, 53
© David Livingston: pp. 9, 19, 31 top, 44, 63 bottom, 67, 68
© Mark Lohman: p. 45
© Peter Paige: p. 41 bottom
© Eric Roth: pp. 10, 16, 23, 31 bottom, 49, 60
© Bill Rothschild: pp. 2, 35 left, 38, 50
© Tim Street-Porter: pp. 6, 14 bottom, 27, 28, 30, 46, 52, 56 left
© Peter Vanderwarker/Gary Wolf Architects: p. 66 top
© Jessie Walker: pp. 15, 18, 26 left, 32
© Paul Warchol: pp. 39 right, 58

INDEX